Routes of
Cross-Cultural
Exchange

Mediterranean Trade Routes

John Micklos Jr.

Cavendish
Square

New York

Published in 2018 by Cavendish Square Publishing, LLC
243 5th Avenue, Suite 136, New York, NY 10016

Copyright © 2018 by Cavendish Square Publishing, LLC

First Edition

Website: cavendishsq.com

This publication represents the opinions and views of the author based on his or her personal experience, knowledge, and research. The information in this book serves as a general guide only. The author and publisher have used their best efforts in preparing this book and disclaim liability rising directly or indirectly from the use and application of this book.

CPSIA Compliance Information: Batch #CS17CSQ

All websites were available and accurate when this book was sent to press.

Library of Congress Cataloging-in-Publication Data

Names: Micklos Jr, John.
Title: Mediterranean trade routes / John Micklos Jr.
Description: New York : Cavendish Square, 2018. | Series: Routes of cross-cultural exchange | Includes index.
Identifiers: ISBN 9781502626936 (library bound) | ISBN 9781502626790 (ebook)
Subjects: LCSH: Trade routes--Mediterranean Region--History--Juvenile literature. | Mediterranean Region--Juvenile literature.
Classification: LCC HE361.M53 2018 | DDC 382'.09--dc23

Editorial Director: David McNamara
Editor: Caitlyn Miller
Copy Editor: Michele Suchomel-Casey
Associate Art Director: Amy Greenan
Designer: Jessica Nevins
Production Coordinator: Karol Szymczuk
Photo Research: J8 Media

The photographs in this book are used by permission and through the courtesy of: Cover, Canaletto (1697–1768)/uploader was Hajotthu at de.wikipedia (http://de.wikipedia.org)/File: Canaletto, Reception French Ambassador Eremitage St. Petersburg 02.JPG/Wikimedia Commons/Public Domain; p. 5 Rainer Lesniewski/Shutterstock.com; p. 8 Brandelet/Shutterstock.com; p. 10 Steven Wright/Shutterstock.com; pp. 14–15 Elzbieta Sekowska/Shutterstock.com; p. 16 Michael Nicholson/Corbis/Getty Images; p. 18 Lampman/Own work/File: Late Medieval Trade Routes.jpg/ Wikimedia Commons/Public Domain; p. 23 De Agostini Picture Library/Getty Images; p. 28 George Rinhart/Corbis/Getty Images; p. 30 Scott Smith/Corbis/Getty Images; pp. 38–39 Photomarine/ Shutterstock.com; p. 40 Vixit/Shutterstock.com; p. 46 en: User: User: Argos'Dad [1] ("http:// en.wikipedia.org/wiki/Image:Constantinople_Mural_Fourth_Crusade.jpg)/"http://en.wikipedia. org/wiki/Image:Constantinople_Mural_Fourth_Crusade.jpg)/File: Constantinople mural, Istanbul Archaeological Museums.jpg/Wikimedia Commons/Public Domain; p. 49 wynnter/E+/Getty Images; pp. 50–51 Heritage Images/Hulton Fine Art Collection/Getty Images; pp. 54–55 Musee Massey, Tarbes, France/Bridgeman Images; p. 56 Samot/Shutterstock.com; p. 60 Kamira/Shutterstock.com; p. 63 Leonardo da Vinci (1452–1519)/Cropped and relevelled from File: Mona Lisa, by Leonardo da Vinci, from C2RMF.jpg. Originally C2RMF: Galerie de tableaux en très haute définition (http:// www.technologies.c2r mf.fr/imaging/showcase/): image page (http://www.technologies.c2rmf.fr/ iipimage/showcase/ zoom/cop29)/File: Mona Lisa, by Leonardo da Vinci, from C2RMF retouched. jpg/Wikimedia Commons/Public Domain; p. 71 Jacques Marais/Gallo Images/Getty Images; p. 72 dr.katsf/Shutterstock.com; p. 76 Federico Rostagno/Shutterstock.com; p. 78 Faraways/Shutterstock. com; p. 80 Christian Mueller/Shutterstock.com; pp. 82–83 Chalalai Atcha/Shutterstock.com; p. 84 Slavko Sereda/Shutterstock.com.

Printed in the United States of America

Table of Contents

Introduction / 4
A Rich History of Trade

Chapter 1 / 9
Trade Before the Mediterranean Trade Routes

Chapter 2 / 17
Foundations and Explorations

Chapter 3 / 31
Goods and Services

Chapter 4 / 41
The Major Players

Chapter 5 / 57
The Effects of the Mediterranean Trade Routes

Chapter 6 / 73
The Future of the Mediterranean Trade Routes

Glossary / 86
Further Information / 88
Bibliography / 90
Index / 92
About the Author / 96

A Rich History of Trade

Silk. Sugar. Spices. Slaves. These are just a few of the trade goods transported across the Mediterranean Sea over the past three thousand years or so. One of the world's oldest trade routes, the Mediterranean remains a vital economic force today. Bordered on the east by Asia, the north by Europe, and the south by Africa, more than twenty countries touch its waters.

The Mediterranean stretches roughly 2,300 miles (3,701.5 kilometers). Syria, Lebanon, and Israel lay on its easternmost points. Spain and Morocco mark its western edges, where it connects with the Atlantic Ocean at the Strait of Gibraltar. Almost completely surrounded by land, the sea merits its Latin name, *mediterraneus*, which means "inland" or "middle of land." Gibraltar's narrow opening—only 9 miles (14 km) wide at its narrowest point—is all that prevents the Mediterranean from complete containment. And while many people think of "oceans" and "seas" as being the same, seas are actually smaller. They tend to be extensions of oceans that are partially enclosed by land. The Mediterranean is an extension of the Atlantic Ocean.

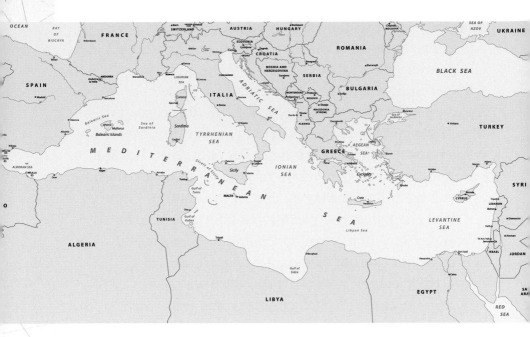

The Mediterranean Sea is bordered by three continents—Europe, Africa, and Asia—and by more than twenty countries.

During its long history, the Mediterranean has been called many names. The Hebrew Bible refers to it as the "Great Sea" or simply the "Sea." The Romans often called it "Our Sea," reflecting the sense of ownership they felt toward its waters. Through the years, many great civilizations had their cultures intertwined with the Mediterranean. More than three thousand years ago, Egyptian ships first ventured into its waters on short voyages. Hugging the coast, they traveled to Palestine and Syria, their nearest neighbors. But, over time, the Egyptian port of Alexandria hosted vessels from across the Mediterranean. Its lighthouse stood as one of the Seven Wonders of the Ancient World.

In the first millennium BCE, Greek and Phoenician sailors crisscrossed the Mediterranean's waters. Classic Greek tales such as the *Odyssey* and the myth of Jason and the Golden Fleece spotlighted the adventure of travel. Coins and other items found in Greek archaeological sites show evidence of trade with far-flung areas. The Greeks even traveled as far as Alexandria. There they gathered silk from the Orient to take back to Greece. As Greek power waned, the Roman Empire rose. For centuries, Roman influence spanned the Mediterranean, and goods from everywhere found their way across the empire.

After the fall of the Western Roman Empire, the Byzantine Empire controlled the Mediterranean for centuries. Its capital, Constantinople, served as a major trade center. Marco Polo's journeys in the late thirteenth century CE opened trade with China. Although the Silk Road trade route went overland, goods then traveled across the Mediterranean on their way to various ports. During the **Renaissance**, Genoa and Venice became key trading **hubs**.

As with empires, the influence of trade routes ebbs and flows over time. In 1488, Portuguese explorer Bartolomeu Dias became the first person to navigate around the Cape of Good Hope at the southernmost tip of Africa. This opened a new route for goods to travel from Asia to the Atlantic Ocean. Still, the Mediterranean remained vital for the many trading partners that lined its shores.

The Mediterranean remained important throughout the twentieth century. During World War I, the sea served as a vital supply route for the Allied forces (France, England, and later, the United States) in their fight against the Axis powers (Germany, Austria/Hungary, and their allies). The sea played an even larger role in World War II, as France, England,

and the United States battled Germany and Italy for control of southern Europe and northern Africa.

After World War II, oil became the prime **commodity** shipped across the Mediterranean. As more and more of the world's oil came from the Middle East, thousands of tankers traveled up the Suez Canal. From there they spread across the Mediterranean and beyond. But war between Egypt and Israel in 1967 closed the canal for several years. By the time it reopened, many oil supertankers had grown too big for the canal. Instead, they traveled around the tip of South Africa with their cargo.

In the twenty-first century, one of the Mediterranean's key commodities is tourism. With its deep blue waters and exotic ports along three continents, the region draws thousands of cruise ships and millions of tourists each year. The Mediterranean ranks among the world's top cruise destinations, with favorite spots including the French Riviera, the Greek islands, Italy, and Spain's Costa del Sol.

One of the world's oldest trade routes, the Mediterranean Sea maintains its importance today. And, given the rich array of countries and ports that line its waters, it is likely to remain a vital part of the region's economy for decades to come.

Chapter 1

Trade Before the Mediterranean Trade Routes

For centuries, transporting goods across North Africa and the Middle East meant traveling across the desert by foot or on a donkey. After camels were **domesticated**, they became the primary means for carrying trade goods. Camels remained important even as ancient civilizations developed boats capable of navigating the deep waters of the Mediterranean Sea.

Different groups have thrived along and near the Mediterranean Sea for more than five thousand years. Considered by many to be the "cradle of civilization," the land of Mesopotamia extended along the Tigris and Euphrates Rivers through what are now Iraq, Kuwait, and eastern Syria. For centuries, many of the people living in the region were **nomads**, roaming from place to place. Over

Opposite: The Great Pyramid was one of the Seven Wonders of the Ancient World. It remains a top tourist attraction today.

Many people consider the region of Mesopotamia to be the "cradle of civilization."

time, greater numbers of people settled into **sedentary** farming. Historians believe that some limited trade took place between the nomads and the farmers.

By 3500 BCE, the Sumerians had developed a series of city-states across the region. Their influence continued for more than a thousand years before starting a gradual decline. The Babylonian and Assyrian empires followed. For the most part, these city-states traded among themselves. Gradually, however, travel and trade from Mesopotamia spread to western Syria and Canaan along the edge of the sea.

Written language originated in this region around 3500 BCE. At roughly the same time, the Sumerians in Mesopotamia and the Egyptians began keeping written records. At first the Sumerians used a system of **pictographs**. In this system, pictures represented the objects being described. For instance, a picture of a boat represented the word "boat." Over time, pictographs evolved into a form of script writing called **cuneiform**.

Meanwhile, the Egyptians developed a system of writing called hieroglyphics. In this system, characters stood for words, syllables, or letters. Scribes recorded these early writings on wood or papyrus, a thick type of paper made from the papyrus plant. Archaeologists have discovered remnants of these writings in tombs and other sites across Egypt. These ancient writings provide insights into how people lived in these early civilizations. They also allowed the exchange of ideas among cultures.

The Pyramids: A Source of Regional Trade

By 2500 BCE, Egypt had formed a mighty empire on the tip of northern Africa. Ruled by a series of pharaohs—both men and women—the Egyptians had a well-formed society. From pharaohs to farmers, from priests to soldiers, from craftsmen to slaves, Egyptians held a wide range of jobs.

Known for their craftsmanship, the Egyptians ranked as the master builders of ancient times. The Great Pyramid and the Great Sphinx of Giza were both built over a period of decades around 2500 BCE. These massive structures seem even more remarkable considering the sheer manpower needed to build them. Ramps and **sledges** represented the only means of technology to move the massive stone blocks into place in the pyramid.

Archaeologists believe that approximately four thousand permanent workers and their families lived in a village beside the pyramid site. As many as twenty thousand more laborers helped at any given time. They lived in a temporary camp near the village and worked for several months at a time. Then a fresh set of workers replaced them. Project managers organized the workforce into divisions of twenty workers and divided the mammoth task into manageable chunks.

The common laborers who lived in the temporary camp did the heavy work of moving the giant blocks of stone that made up the pyramids. Engineers discovered that wetting the sand reduced friction, making it far easier for the groups of workers to pull the huge blocks forward. Day after day, the laborers toiled and sweated under the desert sun. Engineers designed ramps that allowed workers to haul the blocks higher and higher as the pyramid gradually rose over a period of months and years.

For their efforts, the workers received wages of rations, including loaves of bread, meat, and beer. Egyptologists believe they also received pay in the form of others goods or credits that could be used to purchase those goods. All of this meant that the pyramids stimulated regional trade. Boats carried workers, building materials, and other supplies up and down the Nile River. Just feeding the workers required providing thousands of pounds of meat each day. Animal bones excavated from the area show that workers ate ducks, sheep, and pigs. They even ate beef, which had to be transported from areas that had grass for cattle to feed upon. Workers came from all over Egypt, which led to the transfer of culture and trade goods across regions.

Historians know that the massive blocks of limestone in the pyramids at Giza came from across the Nile. The granite in the nearby temples came from hundreds of miles upstream. Sturdy boats would have been needed to transport those heavy loads to the building spot. Archaeologists have also found models of boats in the tombs in many pyramids. They even found a full-size boat near the pyramid erected for the pharaoh Cheops. Clearly, Egypt's early leaders found boats important.

Trade Begins to Span Cultures

For many centuries, there was little trade or cultural exchange between civilizations. The technology of the time did not allow for the construction of boats able to travel across a body of water as wide and deep as the Mediterranean. Even travel up major rivers was limited. Meanwhile, overland travel across the desert presented its own challenges.

The first trade was primarily within cultures. Goods moved up and down the Nile and around the shores of ancient Greece. Gradually, despite the challenges, civilizations began to reach out to one another through travel and trade.

Eventually, societies developed stronger boats capable of ocean travel. These advances set the stage for new trade routes that would link civilizations on all sides of the Mediterranean. These new trade routes allowed the exchange of both merchandise and culture. Those exchanges set the stage for changes that would alter the region forever.

Desert Trade

Imagine a group of merchants crossing the desert on a long string of camels. The sun beats down with temperatures exceeding 100 degrees Fahrenheit (37.7 degrees Celsius). White froth drips from the camels' mouths as they plod along, their broad, flat hooves leaving deep prints in the soft sand. At the end of the day, the camels kneel down, and the merchants dismount. Then the merchants and their helpers unload the bundles of trade goods from the camels' backs and make camp for the night. Their fires burn bright in the cool, starry night as temperatures plummet as much as 50 degrees Fahrenheit (27.8 degrees Celsius) from the daytime highs. At dawn, the merchants break camp and load the

Camels provide reliable transportation across the desert. For many centuries, they played a key role in regional trade.

camels. Then they begin another long day's trek toward the never-changing horizon.

Able to travel several days at a time without water, camels were ideally suited for transporting loads across the desert. A typical caravan might include one thousand camels. Some had ten thousand or more. Large caravans provided protection against desert bandits. A caravan might cover 20 to 30 miles (32.2 km to 48.3 km) in a day. The journey continued for days and even weeks. Camels remained an important means of transporting goods long after trade routes were established across the Mediterranean Sea. Gold, salt, and copper were among the goods transported across the Sahara Desert on camels. Meanwhile, camels carried silk, jade, gold, and other luxury items back and forth along the Silk Road between China and Constantinople.

Chapter 2

Foundations and Explorations

Trade across the Mediterranean Sea did not happen all at once. No one person or single civilization can take credit. Rather, trade evolved bit by bit, route by route, over a period of centuries. As the technologies of shipbuilding improved, sturdier and speedier vessels enabled merchants to visit more distant ports. As navigation improved, allowing **mariners** to sail by night as well as by day, the routes expanded. And as more civilizations in different areas of the Mediterranean became involved in trade, they built on existing routes and established new ones.

Sea trade probably began with short trips connecting nearby ports. Archaeologists have determined that sailors ventured into the waters near Malta and Sicily roughly six thousand years ago. However, they probably only traded with one another or with nearby towns on the Italian mainland.

Opposite: *This eighteenth-century print depicts a trireme. Greeks, Romans, and Phoenicians all used variations of this warship.*

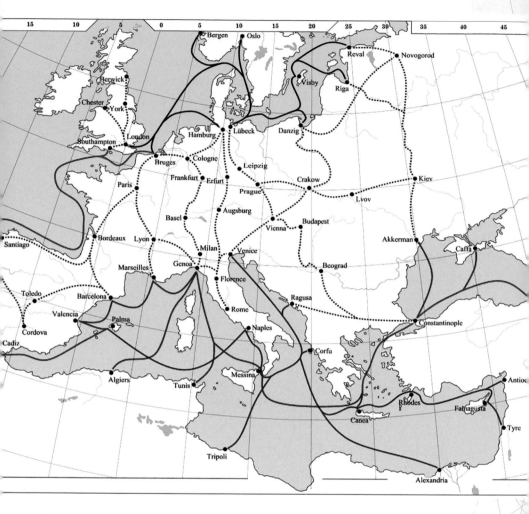

These lines represent just a few of the many trade routes that crisscrossed the Mediterranean over the centuries.

From early in their empire, Egyptian boats traveled up and down the Nile River carrying goods and people. Sometime around 3000 BCE, they ventured out into the sea. A note written during the reign of the pharaoh Snefru referred to a fleet of forty ships loaded with cedar wood arriving from Byblos, a city in Lebanon. The Egyptians were not skilled sailors, however, and they never fully adapted their ships for ocean travel. Their trade was largely restricted to Palestine and Syria, whose cities lay only a few hundred miles away. They also traveled north across the open sea to the island of Crete, which lay around 400 miles (643.7 km) away.

Across the Mediterranean, the Minoans formed a strong civilization on the island of Crete around 2000 BCE. The Minoans became known for the magnificent palaces they built and for exporting lumber. From Crete, their lumber traveled to Egypt, Syria, Cyprus, the Aegean Islands, and mainland Greece.

Evolving Ships

The first boats to venture out into the Mediterranean's waters were simple crafts. They consisted of dugout logs or rafts crafted from reeds. Sailors stayed close to shore—these boats were not built for long voyages across many miles of open sea. They would not have been able to handle winds, waves, or storms. Furthermore, sailors had no tools for navigation. That made sailing at night almost impossible.

Early Egyptian boats were made of planks, either woven together or fastened with wooden pegs. They used papyrus reeds or grass to seal the joints and keep water out. Egyptian ships used both wind power and people power for **propulsion**. They used a row of oarsmen and a mast with a single square sail. To enhance power and speed, the Egyptians later added another row of oarsmen. Their ships proved difficult to navigate on the open sea, however.

When constructing vessels, most ancient shipbuilders started with the outside of the boat and worked their way inside. They started by constructing the hull; then they built the insides of the ship.

Over time, civilizations along the northern and eastern shores of the Mediterranean broadened the scope of travel and trade. The Phoenicians and Greeks brought trade to a whole new level, greatly expanding the markets. Their merchants traveled to Spain, Egypt, and Italy. Meanwhile, Athens became a trading hub for goods from throughout the Mediterranean region.

Around 600 BCE, the Greeks began developing specialized cargo ships. The first cargo vessels weighed about 150 tons (136 tonnes), but later versions grew to about 400 tons (362.8 tonnes). These ships traveled slowly, but they could carry large loads of trade goods. They used both sails and oars for propulsion.

The Greeks protected their trade routes with a fleet of warships called **triremes**; the word means "with three banks of oars." Phoenicians, Greeks, and Romans all used this type of long and slender **galley**. Although they had sails, triremes were propelled primarily by manpower. Rows of oars ran the length of the boat on both sides in three tiers. A trireme might have had as many as 170 rowers. These warships battled by ramming their opponents. They could travel up to 9 or 10 knots (10 or 11 miles per hour), and skilled sailors could maneuver them easily.

Galleys remained in use throughout the Middle Ages. Because Mediterranean winds are often unpredictable, ships that could be propelled by oars as well as sails were preferred both for trading and as warships. Also, most long-distance commerce was conducted between March and October. Winter winds and storms made the seas much more dangerous from November through February.

Improved Navigation

In order to expand their sailing ranges, ancient mariners needed to improve their methods of navigation. Navigating at night, when there were no land features in sight, provided special challenges. The Phoenicians became experts at using the sky for guidance. By day, they marked the progress of the sun from east to west. At night, they read the stars. Observing their location in relation to Polaris, the North Star, helped them determine their location and direction. In fact, ancient writers referred to Polaris as the "Phoenician Star."

Soon after the birth of Christ, sailors began using charts. The ancient Greeks used a **periplus**. This simple document gave a listing of ports and coastal landmarks, along with approximate distances in between. The information came from reports provided by sailors after their travels. In the second century, Ptolemy of Alexandria created the world's first atlas: it included twenty-seven maps. The most reliable ones focused on the areas of Mediterranean that had been well explored. Over the centuries, maps and charts grew more detailed and reliable as sailors gathered further information during their travels. By the thirteenth century, full-fledged maps prepared to scale helped guide sailors.

Eventually, sailors developed more sophisticated technology. Around the tenth century, Arabian mariners introduced the astrolabe and the quadrant. The astrolabe allowed sailors to determine direction by finding the time of the rising and setting of the sun, along with the altitude of the sun and selected stars. The quadrant is an instrument used to measure angles. Mariners used it to mark the observed altitude of Polaris when they entered a port of call. Then they kept those figures to guide them the next time they visited the area.

Meanwhile, the Chinese had been using a form of compass for centuries. Over time, it made its way to the Mediterranean, possibly by way of the Silk Road. Although the compass was first mentioned in Western writing in 1187, it took many decades before the instrument was used widely. Some superstitious sailors believed the compass brought bad luck.

Another key advance came around 1730 with the invention of the sextant. Sailors had been able to find their latitude (points north or south of the equator) for centuries. But determining longitude (points east or west of the Prime Meridian) was impossible. The sextant (and later the octant) allowed mariners to easily determine their longitude. Sextants and octants remained popular until the twentieth century. Then sailors could use radio and telegraph signals to determine their location. Today, sailors use a Global Positioning System (GPS) device for immediate and precisely accurate information about location.

Lighting the Way: Ancient Lighthouses

For thousands of years, lighthouses have guided sailors safely into ports. One of the most famous structures of ancient times, the Lighthouse at Alexandria stood as the tallest structure in the world, other than the Great Pyramid. Built over a period of about twenty years beginning in 290 BCE, it earned a place on the Greeks' list of the Seven Wonders of the Ancient World.

The Lighthouse at Alexandria guided ships for more than a thousand years.

A large fire burned constantly at the top of the lighthouse, and a curved mirror projected the light from the fire into a beam. Supposedly, ships could see the light of the fire at night and the smoke of the fire during the day at a distance of 100 miles (160.9 km). The lighthouse stood as a beacon to visiting ships for more than one thousand years. An earthquake in 1303 damaged the lighthouse, and it finally collapsed a few decades later.

The Greeks and Romans built a number of lighthouses at key points around the Mediterranean and beyond. Some of these lighthouses operated for centuries. For instance, Rome built the Tower of Hercules lighthouse in northwest Spain in the first century CE. That lighthouse still stands today, although it has been extensively repaired and renovated.

Evolving Routes

There was no single Mediterranean trade route. Rather, routes evolved and changed over the centuries. The routes changed as the dominant civilizations in the region changed. The major trade routes revolved around each culture's key ports. Routes also grew and spread as the need for goods and services changed. Egyptian routes centered on the southern and eastern regions of the sea.

Based on Crete, Minoan sailors extended the existing trade routes. They went south to Egypt and east to the Levant, where Lebanon, Syria, and Israel are now. The early Greeks took over the Minoan routes. They also traded with partners throughout the Aegean Sea. These included Troy on the western tip of Asia. This then opened trade through the Black Sea as well.

Around 1500 BCE, the Phoenicians entered the scene. They set up colonies on Cyprus and Rhodes, but they explored even farther. Because they used the stars for navigation, Phoenicians could sail at night, which greatly extended the area they could cover. They traveled the entire breadth of the Mediterranean as far west as what is now Spain. They also founded trading posts and colonies along the North African coast as far west as Tangier. Once Carthage was established in northern Tunisia, it became one of the great cities of the ancient world.

While the Phoenicians focused on the southern portion of the Mediterranean, the Greeks focused more on the northern areas. They traded to the east with Tarsus and Cyprus. They traveled west to Italy, Sicily, and Sardinia. They did go south to Crete, and they even traveled to Egypt on the northern coast of Africa. They also went northeast to Troy and into the Black

Sea. Between the Phoenicians and the Greeks, most of the Mediterranean was opened to trade by the time of Christ.

Through their conquests, the Romans extended the trade network even farther. From their central location in the northern Mediterranean, they could reach as far west as Spain and as far south and east as Egypt and Canaan within about twenty days. Traveling overland within these countries took longer, however.

After the Roman Empire split around 285 CE, the western portion faded. The Eastern Empire, however, thrived. Known as the Byzantine Empire, it was based in Constantinople. Strategically located at the intersection of Europe and Asia, the city became a thriving trading center. Merchants came from the cities of Genoa and Venice to trade. Others came from Asia. By 500 CE, Constantinople ranked as the world's largest city, with a population of approximately five hundred thousand. Yet goods and merchants did not just come into Constantinople; they went out as well. Trade routes extended across the northern Mediterranean east to Cyprus. Merchants also traveled to the west to Rome and Venice.

One important trade route that greatly impacted the Mediterranean region was an overland route that did not even extend all the way to the Mediterranean Sea. The Silk Road—named centuries later for its most famous commodity—stretched nearly 5,000 miles (8,046.7 km) from the eastern part of China to Constantinople, where silk, tea, and other goods from China made their way to other ports across the Mediterranean. Other goods traveled south across Syria to Alexandria. From there trade routes continued south through Egypt or west across northern Africa.

The Silk Road had been operating for more than one thousand years when Marco Polo of Venice first traveled along it to Asia in 1271. Just seventeen years old, he made the journey with his father and uncle. After reaching China, Marco Polo stayed for twenty-four years. Although other Europeans had visited Asia before, Marco Polo drew widespread notice to its wonders. He wrote the stories of his travels, stirring people's imaginations. His stories also stimulated demand for exotic goods that were not otherwise available.

As the Renaissance blossomed between 1300 and 1600, trade centered around Italian city-states such as Genoa and Venice. Centrally located along the northern Mediterranean, these towns became important hubs for the east-west flow of goods from Greece and Constantinople to the rising western European powers France and Spain. In fact, Venice ranked as one of the most prosperous cities in Europe at that time. It controlled most of the maritime trade in that part of the Mediterranean.

A Changing Balance of Power

By the 1500s, several things had happened that changed the balance of power surrounding the Mediterranean. In 1453, the Ottomans captured Constantinople, ending the Byzantine Empire. They now controlled the rich trade of silk and spices that passed through the city. They began charging huge taxes on trade goods before they moved west. The Venetians and others began looking for alternate routes that would allow trade goods from Asia to bypass Constantinople.

The wish for a new route was granted later in the fifteenth century. In 1488, Portuguese sailor Bartolomeu Dias crossed the Cape of Good Hope at the southern tip of Africa. In 1497, countryman Vasco da Gama extended the journey by traveling from the Atlantic Ocean around the cape. He then continued up the eastern coast of Africa and across the Indian Ocean to India. This opened up a new way for people in Europe to get goods from Asia.

Meanwhile, by the early 1500s, explorations by Christopher Columbus and others had opened up the New World of North and South America. Soon ships from Spain, Portugal, France, England, and other European countries were crisscrossing the Atlantic Ocean for trade and conquest. This new focus reduced reliance on the traditional Mediterranean trade routes. It effectively ended the dominance of powers such as Venice and Constantinople and shifted influence to the rising powers of western Europe over the next several centuries. The Mediterranean remained important for regional trade, but it had less global influence.

The opening of the Suez Canal in 1869 once again raised the profile of Mediterranean trade routes. Going up the Suez Canal from the Red Sea to the Mediterranean Sea and across to the Atlantic Ocean cut thousands of miles off the trip around the southern tip of Africa. With the booming oil trade of the twentieth century, the Mediterranean regained prominence as a key to international trade—at least for a while.

In the twenty-first century, trade has become truly global. There is much less reliance on any single trade route or network. Despite all of the changes, however, Mediterranean trade routes have remained important throughout the centuries, and they remain vital today.

Obstacles of the Sea

Sailing the Mediterranean Sea in ancient times presented many challenges. In the waters off of western North Africa, gale force storms sometimes blow in from the Atlantic Ocean. Farther east, strong north winds from Europe sometimes blow so fiercely that they create waterspouts. Even today, the Mediterranean offers the most favorable sailing conditions

The Greek legend of Scylla and Charybdis described the dangers of navigating certain areas of the Mediterranean.

between late spring and early fall because the seas are rougher during the winter.

The Greeks traveled far and wide across the Mediterranean. Skilled sailors, they respected the power of the sea and created legends about its dangers. Homer's *Odyssey* describes the dangers of Scylla and Charybdis. Scylla was portrayed as a female monster: her six heads, perched on snakelike necks, lashed out with razor-sharp teeth to devour any sailors who passed too near her. Charybdis was on the opposite shore of the narrow channel; she swallowed unsuspecting ships that ventured too close to her whirlpool-like waters. This legend led to the saying "caught between Scylla and Charybdis." That means having two choices, both of which are not ideal.

Experts believe that the legend relates to a real-life area. The narrow Strait of Messina separates Sicily and mainland Italy. Sharp rocks, coupled with strong and shifting currents, create challenges for sailors even today. Furthermore, ancient sailors had no navigational equipment—they had only the sun and stars to guide them. Despite the dangers of long-distance sea voyages, ancient sailors gradually ventured farther and farther. This generated the exchange of goods and culture across civilizations.

Chapter 3

Goods and Services

Throughout their long history, Mediterranean trade routes have carried a rich and varied array of goods over the years. Some of these items have had particular influence on the region. Tin, grains, silk, slaves, and more helped to alter the course of ancient history. Today, crude and refined oil, as well as fish, are goods that shape modern trade relationships.

Tin

Tin ranked as one of the top commodities during the Bronze Age, which started around 3300 BCE and lasted more than two thousand years. Early civilizations such as Egypt discovered that bronze

Opposite: *This bronze drum dates to the seventh century BCE and today is part of the Heraklion Archeological Museum's collection.*

weapons and tools were sturdier and more powerful than ones made with copper or stone. Making bronze is a process. It involves mixing tin and copper to create a bronze **alloy**. In today's world, tin is an inexpensive metal used in many alloys and as a plating to protect steel from corrosion. During the Bronze Age, tin was a precious metal desperately needed to create bronze.

Tin deposits were fairly rare in the ancient world. Furthermore, many of these deposits were far removed from where civilizations were located. Some minor deposits lay in what is now Italy. Others lay farther away—in Spain, England, and Germany. Even after mining the tin, delivering it to where it would be used could take weeks. Some of it traveled overland while some traveled by ship from ports on the northern shores of the Mediterranean. The search for tin, coupled with the development of better long-range boats and sailing techniques, helped spur the rapid expansion of trade.

For instance, the island of Crete became a center for the making of bronze. The Minoans who lived there became the first strong European civilization. They thrived from roughly 3000 BCE until 1650 BCE. Over time, Minoan ships ranged as far as Spain in search of tin, which they brought back to make bronze. Other tin came overland from European sources.

Minoan sailors also traveled south across the Mediterranean to trade with Egypt. They also traded with the Phoenicians, who lived along the eastern edge of the sea in what are now Syria, Lebanon, and Israel. Archaeologists have found artifacts from ancient Minoan palaces that prove this type of long-distance trade existed.

Wheat and Grain

Grain was the motor that ran the ancient world. Grain fed both workers and animals; without access to grain, civilizations could not survive. Small wonder, then, that for centuries grain was an important trade commodity. For instance, between 1000 and 500 BCE, the Greeks traded extensively with ports across the Mediterranean. From their homeland, the Greeks exported olive oil and wine. They also traded pottery and items made of metal. Wheat and barley were major imports because Greeks needed the wheat to make food.

Wheat and grain also served as key commodities in war. Many ancient cities had sturdy walls. Often, they were strategically located to make a direct assault by land or sea difficult. Over time, generals learned how to conquer cities by conducting **sieges**. By strategically cutting off supplies of grain, an invading army could starve the inhabitants of a city into submission. Likewise, the invaders might burn the crops outside the city. This would force the army inside the city to either come out and fight or surrender.

The timing of wars also revolved around crops. Often, armies had to disband as the harvest season approached. In fact, there were no professional armies until the time of the Roman Empire—soldiers were generally farmers. They needed to return to their fields to gather the harvest. Likewise, the nation needed the grain that the harvest would provide.

Silk

Contact with China, India, and other Asian cultures brought a new set of products to civilizations throughout the Mediterranean region. From the East came tea, porcelain, sugar, salt, and other spices. The most important commodity gave the trade route its name—the Silk Road. In exchange for silk, traders from the West delivered gold, silver, and ivory, as well as food items such as pomegranates.

The Silk Road began in the eastern part of China. From there it wound its way overland to various points, including Constantinople. A round trip along its entire length could take two years. Because the journey was so long and expensive, traders preferred to carry luxury goods that could generate the biggest profits, such as silk. But merchants rarely made the entire journey. Sometimes they met other merchants at various points along the route to make their deals. Sometimes middlemen would serve as brokers for the deals.

Of all the products to travel along the Silk Road, silk probably had the greatest influence on the cultures it reached. Strong yet lightweight, silk revolutionized fashion worldwide. Because it was at first scarce and expensive, wearing silk served as a mark of wealth or nobility. The Romans prized silk highly. At first, only emperors and wealthy people wore it. Over time, however, its use spread. In the fourth century, Roman historian Ammianus Marcellinus wrote, "The use of silk was once confined to the nobility, but it has now spread to all classes without distinction, even to the lowest people."

For centuries, the Chinese carefully guarded the silkworms that created the raw silk. Therefore, for centuries they had a **monopoly** on the silk trade. Eventually, though, silkworms were smuggled out of China. Gradually, the silk industry grew in other

Buying Through Barter

Although coins existed as a form of buying from before the start of the Common Era, much of the trade in the ancient world was conducted by barter. Greek historian Herodotus described how merchants from Carthage bartered on the coast of Morocco. They unloaded their cargo on the beach and went back aboard their ships to light a fire. Seeing the smoke, nearby traders came to view the cargo. Then they laid down gold as payment and backed away. The traders from Carthage came and examined the gold. If they thought the price was fair, they took the gold and left the goods. If not, they returned to their ships. Then the local people would add more gold until both sides agreed that the price was fair.

This system required trust on both sides. In theory, one side or the other could simply try to run off with the other's goods. But in practice, the exchanges generally went well. Both sides felt they had made a fair deal, which is the ultimate way to judge an effective barter exchange.

places. Even today, silk remains a valuable commodity. Between them, China and Japan produce more than half of the world's silk each year.

The Silk Road remained an important trade route for centuries. Eventually, as ocean routes to China were discovered, it lost some of its luster. By the end of the fifteenth century, the Silk Road was no longer a major trade route.

Slaves

Slavery was not as important in the Mediterranean region as in many other parts of the world. Still, slavery played a role in Mediterranean trade. In the thirteenth century, Catalonia became a major trader in the region. Catalan ships traveled across the Mediterranean Sea from Spain to Africa. They carried grain and cloth to ports along northern Africa. For those goods, the Africans traded gold, wool, dried fruits, and slaves.

Sugar and Spices

Humans have had a "sweet tooth" almost since the beginning of time. That made sugar a popular trade good for many centuries. By the twelfth century, Egypt and Syria had become major producers. In the later Middle Ages, Cyprus established large sugar plantations. After 1400, Spain and Sicily became major producers. During all of this time, trade in sugar occurred throughout the Mediterranean. Similarly, spices were rare and precious commodities. Salt is the most basic and probably oldest of the spices. Civilizations along the Mediterranean have produced sea salt through evaporation for thousands of years. To illustrate just how valuable salt was, Roman soldiers were sometimes paid in salt. In fact, that's where the word "salary" comes from.

Other spices were important commodities as well. The Silk Road opened the trade of spices from China. Silk Road merchants brought trade in cinnamon, ginger, pepper, cardamom, and other spices. Spices were so precious in the ancient world that at one point nutmeg was more valuable than an equivalent weight of gold.

Modern Trade Goods

Commercial Fishing

In recent years, commercial fishing has become an important regional industry in the Mediterranean. Sardines are plentiful in the western and northeastern areas of the Mediterranean, and anchovy can be found in most regions of the sea. The bluefin tuna is another important commercial catch. Other top commercial fish species include flounder, turbot, sea bass, soles, and whitings. Most of the trade in fish is local or regional in nature.

Oil

In the same way that wheat and other grains ran the ancient world, oil runs the modern world. Societies use it to run cars, trains, and airplanes, and for heat. Without oil, most engines would cease to run. Small wonder, then, that in today's world oil is one of the most important trade commodities.

In modern times, oil has been one of the prime commodities crossing the Mediterranean.

Several countries along the coast of Africa boast significant oil deposits. Algeria, Angola, and Libya all rank among the world's twenty top-producing oil nations. Oil plays an important part in their economies. Countries export oil in order to import other goods they need. Therefore, oil production affects the entire region. Some of the oil gets shipped to other countries that touch the Mediterranean. Other oil gets shipped across the sea to distant countries.

Since the middle of the twentieth century oil has reigned as the prime commodity. Tankers loaded with oil from the Middle East traveled up the Suez Canal. From there they crossed the Mediterranean. Some delivered oil to ports along its shores. Others continued their journeys across the Atlantic Ocean to North and South America. Today, many Middle Eastern oil tankers use ocean routes rather than going through the Suez Canal, but the Mediterranean continues to host significant oil traffic. Furthermore, refineries in Mediterranean ports process large quantities of crude oil from the Middle East.

Chapter 4

The Major Players

Over the centuries, many civilizations and people have played a role in establishing and refining the trade routes spanning the Mediterranean Sea. As civilizations rose and fell, the dominant players in trade changed. At some points in history, dominant powers overlapped. In those cases, sometimes they traded peacefully. Other times, they battled for power.

The Egyptians

The first recorded trading venture into the Mediterranean Sea occurred in 2650 BCE. In that year, forty ships arrived in Egypt. These ships carried a load of lumber from the famous cedar forests of Lebanon, several hundred miles away, for the pharaoh Snefru. Almost certainly, trade had

Opposite: The Egyptians left behind artwork and writing showing various aspects of their culture.

occurred on the sea earlier, but this record offers the first written proof.

Although a succession of pharaohs led a mighty empire over many centuries, they made limited use of the Mediterranean for trade. Queen Hatshepsut, who ruled from 1478 to 1458 BCE, had an ocean voyage depicted on a wall of her tomb. Artwork showed a small fleet of ships arriving in Egypt from a long voyage. The hieroglyphics tell us that the cargo included ebony, myrrh, ivory, gold, and even a live panther. These items likely came from Ethiopia or Somalia.

In general, however, Egyptians never made extensive use of ocean travel. Although they were skilled engineers capable of building massive pyramids, they never built large fleets of ships capable of long-distance ocean travel. Perhaps they felt they had most of the materials they needed within the borders of their own country. Or perhaps they were focused on their own accomplishments, such as building the pyramids.

Interestingly, Egypt again became a major player in Mediterranean trade in the nineteenth and twentieth centuries. With the completion of the Suez Canal in 1869, Egypt controlled the vital connection between the Mediterranean Sea and Red Sea. In the middle of the twentieth century, the canal became the major route for oil produced in the Middle East.

Minoans

The Minoans had one of the great Bronze Age civilizations. They were also the first culture in the Mediterranean region to make extensive use of the sea for trading. Between around 2000 and 1646 BCE, their skilled sailors carried lumber, olive oil, and other exports to Egypt, Syria, Cyprus, the Aegean Islands, and mainland Greece.

Many great civilizations have gradually faded from power over a period of centuries. For the Minoans, the end came suddenly and without warning. Around 1650 BCE, a giant volcano named Thera erupted on the island of Santorini, about 50 miles (80.5 km) away from Crete. Geologists believe it exploded with the power of several hundred atomic bombs. It wiped out the port at Santorini, which housed much of the Minoan fleet. Tsunami waves rushed across the sea and heavily damaged much of Crete. The devastating volcano, followed by years of poor weather for crops, doomed the Minoans. Within fifty years, their civilization had faded.

Phoenicians

Between around 1500 and 300 BCE, the Phoenicians created an empire built almost entirely on trade. Based in Byblos, Sidon, and Tyre on the shores of what is now Lebanon, they sailed and traded along the northern coast of Africa as far west as Tangier. They also traveled to Crete, Sicily, and Sardinia. The Phoenicians established colonies in many spots along their trade routes. One of these colonies, Carthage, became one of the great trade centers of ancient times.

The Phoenicians often acted as middlemen. They brought raw materials from the West. These included wheat, wine, and tin. Then they traded with the civilizations of the East. They added some of the own products, such as timber from the famous cedar forests of Lebanon.

Greeks

Around the same time, the Greek culture flourished in Greece and surrounding areas. Between 776 and 146 BCE, the Greeks erected beautiful temples in Athens and other cities. They established a government that allowed representation by many different individuals, which stands as an early example of democratic principles.

The Greeks also served as key players in regional trade across the Mediterranean. At first, most of their trading was local with neighboring city-states. Often, they colonized their trading partners. Over time, they developed a series of independent city-states across the Mediterranean. By 500 BCE, the Greek empire included roughly five hundred colonies with as many as sixty thousand Greek citizens living in them. These colonies offered possibilities for the exchange of cultures as well as goods.

The seaport colonies also provided opportunities to gather resources and establish trade inland. Some of the colonies became rich and powerful in their own right. Syracuse, located on the east coast of Sicily, was founded as a Greek colony in 734 BCE. At one point, Syracuse boasted the largest army in Greece. The city also served as a cultural center.

Romans

The city of Rome was founded in 753 BCE, and over time the Roman Empire became the dominant civilization in the Mediterranean region. In 509 BCE Rome established a republic, ruled by senators. Julius Caesar became the first emperor of Rome in 45 BCE, effectively ending democracy there. For more than four hundred years, Roman power and influence continued to grow.

From its beginnings, the Roman Empire focused on expansion. First, it defeated Greece. Rome battled with Carthage for more than a century before conquering it in 146 BCE. Carthage gave the Roman Empire a foothold in Africa. From there, Roman conquest spread quickly. By the time of the birth of Christ, Rome controlled all of northern Africa. It had conquered Egypt and **annexed** Hispania (what we now call Spain). Rome controlled Greece and most of Europe. The Romans invaded as far north as England. They also held much of the land in the Middle East.

At its peak around 100 CE, the Roman Empire stretched from Britain in the northwest to Egypt in the southeast. Roman territory covered roughly the size of the continental United States today. The Mediterranean served as the hub for its conquests and its vast trading network. Roman control of the sea's waters allowed it to move soldiers, supplies, and goods from one end of its empire to the other quickly and efficiently. Ocean travel allowed the Romans to reach ports in most of their regions within a week or two. Reaching the inland areas took much longer.

By 285 CE, the Roman Empire had grown so large that it was difficult to manage. In that year, Diocletian split the empire into eastern and western sections. The western section fell in 476 CE when Romulus, the last of the Roman emperors, was defeated by a Germanic army. The eastern section, known as Byzantium, thrived for nearly a thousand years more. Its capital of Constantinople served as a major world trade center. The Turks conquered the city in 1453.

For more than one thousand years, Constantinople, shown in this mural, thrived as a center for trade.

Byzantines

For more than one thousand years, the Byzantine Empire controlled much of the trade in the Mediterranean. This civilization began as an outgrowth of the Roman Empire. In 330 CE, Roman emperor Constantine I decided to found a "New Rome" where the former Greek colony of Byzantium had stood. He named the capital city of this Eastern Roman Empire Constantinople.

Constantinople's location made it a perfect spot to thrive as trade between regions continued to grow. It stood at the intersection of Europe and Asia and marked one of the end points of the famed Silk Road trade route. For centuries, silk stood as the top commodity coming into Constantinople. But many other trade goods passed through Constantinople as well. These included pottery, marble, and a variety of copper and brass items. Over time, Constantinople became one of the world's largest and wealthiest cities. By 1000 CE, its population stood at around six hundred thousand.

Venetians

Many cities across Italy served as trade centers between 1300 and 1600 CE. Venice ranked as perhaps the greatest. The Venetians and, to a slightly lesser degree, the Genoans, controlled much of the trade across the northern Mediterranean throughout the Renaissance. Their trading partners extended as far north as England and as far east as Asia.

The Venetians used a fleet of sleek merchant ships to carry goods throughout the Mediterranean. They transformed the traditional galley into a ship that relied on sails rather than oars for propulsion. These vessels could carry an impressive 250 tons (226.8 tonnes) of cargo. The average life of a galley was ten years, so the Venetian government kept busy constantly updating its fleet.

Venetian power peaked late in the fifteenth century. It began to fade after Portuguese explorers discovered a way to travel around the Cape of Good Hope in South Africa. This ocean route allowed traders transporting goods from Asia to western Europe to avoid the Mediterranean altogether.

People

It wasn't just civilizations that played key roles in the development of trade across the Mediterranean Sea. Groups of people and individuals did, too.

Explorers

Daring explorations played a major role in Greek myths and legends. One early myth centers on the adventures of Jason and his band of Argonauts as they seek to retrieve the legendary Golden Fleece of a ram. Homer's epic tales the *Iliad* and the *Odyssey* spotlight the travels of mighty warrior Odysseus as he returns home following the Trojan War. During his decade-long journey, he was twice shipwrecked, encountered a Cyclops, and survived many other adventures. The Trojan War was a real Bronze Age conflict between Troy and early Greece, which happened around 1200 BCE. Historians long believed Odysseus to be a mythical figure, but now some believe he may have been a real person whose exploits got exaggerated when retold to the point that he seemed larger than life.

Around 515 BCE, King Darius I of Persia sent Greek navigator Scylax to explore the Indus River. Scylax traced the river from its roots in Tibet to where it spills into the Arabian Sea. From there he traveled up the Red Sea and then into the Mediterranean Sea. His travels added much to ancient knowledge about geography.

In 1271, seventeen-year-old Marco Polo began an epic journey with his father and uncle from Venice, Italy, to Asia. After stopping in Persia, they continued overland along what would become known as the Silk

Marco Polo's travels to China helped spark trade that shaped the Mediterranean region for centuries.

Road. After three years of travel, they arrived at the palace of Kublai Khan in China. The Polos remained in Asia for more than twenty years, serving in various capacities. During that time, Marco Polo made several trips to various points throughout China. When the Polos returned to Venice, Marco brought remarkable tales of the wealth he had seen in China; his stories helped stir interest in Asia and Asian goods.

Pirates

Trade across the seas brought wealth. It brought ships laden with gold, silk, spices, and other precious cargo. It also brought pirates. Pirates have threatened merchant ships ever since the beginning of ocean trade; this held true in the Mediterranean Sea as well.

An Egyptian clay tablet from the fourteenth century BCE detailed how pirates attacked ships near the coast of Egypt. Furthermore, pirates did not restrict their activities to the open seas. They sometimes attacked port cities as well. They **pillaged** goods and captured slaves. Sometimes cities paid tributes to the pirates so that they would stay away. However, this practice simply made the pirates richer, bolder, and even more powerful.

Not everyone considered pirates to be a menace. In many areas, pirates were considered "hunters" rather than thieves. One Greek historian noted that among some groups, employment as a pirate "did not yet involve any disgrace, but rather brought with it somewhat of glory." Even the mighty Roman Empire tolerated pirates because they brought a steady stream of captured slaves to Roman ports. Also, fear of pirates created an unsteady market for goods such as grain. This kept prices high, which benefited those who sold it.

The most feared pirates of all were the Barbary pirates, who roamed the Mediterranean, primarily along the coast of northern Africa near Morocco, Algeria, and Libya. Pirates had operated in the region for centuries, but the Barbary pirates reached the

The Barbary pirates, depicted in this painting, were the most famous and feared pirates to roam the Mediterranean.

height of their power in the 1600s. They terrorized merchant ships and towns along the North African coast, but they went farther afield as well, conducting raids up the Atlantic Ocean as far north as Ireland and

The Travels of Marco Polo

Marco Polo's tales of his journey to China in the late thirteenth century spurred European demand for exotic trade goods from that far-off land. Here is an excerpt from *The Book of Ser Marco Polo: The Venetian Concerning Kingdoms and Marvels of the East, Volumes I and II* that describes the Palace of the Great Kaan:

> You must know that it is the greatest palace that ever was … The roof is very lofty, and the walls of the Palace are all covered with gold and silver. They are also adorned with representations of dragons [sculptured and gilt], beasts and birds, knights and idols, and sundry other subjects. And on the ceiling too you see nothing but gold and silver and painting.
>
> [On each of the four sides there is a great marble staircase leading to the top of the marble wall, and forming the approach to the palace.] The Hall of the Palace is so large that it could easily dine 6000 people; and it is quite a marvel to see how many rooms there are besides. The building is altogether so vast, so rich, and so beautiful, that no man on earth could design anything superior to it.

Historians debate the accuracy of Marco Polo's accounts. Some believe he may not have seen as much of China as he claimed. They note that he didn't mention several key aspects of Chinese culture. Other historians point out that he couldn't remember or write about every detail of his travels.

even Iceland. Piracy continued in the area until the early 1800s.

Sailors

Ancient sailors ventured out onto the open sea with nothing to guide them but the sun and stars. They faced danger and possible death each day. Sudden storms might sink them. Unseen rocks near the coast might shipwreck them. Pirates might attack them. Despite all this, these brave mariners explored new waters and opened new trade routes.

Sailors from each civilization and stage of development added something to the overall knowledge of the sea. The Egyptians created the mighty Lighthouse at Alexandria, and centuries later the Romans spread lighthouses across the Mediterranean. The Phoenicians learned to navigate by the stars, making it possible to travel safely at night. The Greeks created the first naval charts, which over the centuries became more and more detailed and accurate. Through trade, western mariners were introduced to the Chinese compass. That instrument greatly improved navigation.

Sailors passed on their wisdom from generation to generation. Over the centuries, this accumulated knowledge made sea travel both faster and safer. This contributed to the establishment of trade routes across wider and wider expanses of the Mediterranean.

Merchants

Without merchants, there can be no trade. Civilizations create trade goods through farmers, artists, and

In medieval times, most merchants operated in small shops, from stands in the street, or by traveling along with their goods.

craftspeople. Sailors transport the goods across the sea to far-flung ports. But it's the merchants who make the whole process run.

In ancient and medieval times, trade was difficult and dangerous work. Some merchants had shops or

stalls in a village. Many, however, traveled with their products, whether those products were silk, spices, pottery, or grain. It might take weeks or months to cross overland routes. A journey along the length of the Silk Road might take as long as two years. Traveling by ocean brought the dangers of storms or shipwrecks. Merchants also might face robbers or pirates eager to steal their goods.

Sometimes, merchants acted as middlemen. For instance, because of the distance, merchants rarely traveled the entire length of the Silk Road. Instead, they sold their trade goods to middlemen who moved them farther along. This process might repeat itself multiple times before the goods reached their final destination.

Considering the length of time Mediterranean trade routes have operated, it's not surprising that many different civilizations and types of people have been major players in Mediterranean trade over the centuries. They all contributed to the rich history of the region.

Chapter 5

The Effects of the Mediterranean Trade Routes

Of all the world's trade routes, routes across the Mediterranean Sea may have had the longest-lasting and deepest effects on the most people. Dating back to the earliest periods of recorded time, trade across the Mediterranean Sea has had profound effects on the region. These effects began from the time that Egyptians first ventured out onto the sea's waters and continue even today. Effects included cultural and religious exchanges, trade, lifestyle changes, and conquest.

Cultural Influences

Before the opening of Mediterranean trade routes, different civilizations had limited interactions. The difficulties of overland travel across long

Opposite: The Parthenon in Athens stands as an example of classical Greek architecture.

distances prevented the easy exchange of culture. And civilizations across the water from one another had no interchanges at all.

That all changed as sea travel became more practical. Egyptian explorations and trade led to more interaction between the Egyptian culture of North Africa and the culture of the Asian people who lived in what is now Lebanon. These interactions affected people's lives in a variety of areas. In a few areas, however, the exchanges brought especially significant changes.

Written Language

One key effect of increased interaction among cultures was the spread of written language. As the Egyptians ventured out into the Mediterranean and as their caravans crossed the deserts, other cultures became exposed to Egyptian hieroglyphics.

Later, the Phoenicians also developed a written alphabet based on letters representing consonants. At the height of Phoenicia's power, around 1200 to 800 BCE, Phoenician traders traveled throughout the entire Mediterranean. In addition to spreading trade goods, they spread their writing system. In fact, many modern alphabets trace their roots to the Phoenician script. These include Arabic, Hebrew, Latin, and Greek scripts.

The development of written language marks one of the hallmark moments in human development. The ability to transmit information through writing changed the way people lived. As farms grew larger, writing played an important role in keeping track of the number of animals and the amount of feed needed for them. Farmers also could keep track of weather patterns and rainfall amounts.

Written language helped support the growth of cities as well. As larger groups of people lived together, societies created written sets of rules for people to live by. City officials also could keep account of the amount of food on hand. In this way, they could ensure that stores were sufficient to meet people's needs. Written documents also described how the government should run.

Furthermore, written language played a role in the development and spread of religion. Writing down religious beliefs and stories allowed priests and other leaders to standardize prayers and rules. The Egyptian word "hieroglyphics" can be translated to mean "language of the Gods," showing just how important they thought hieroglyphics were. The Egyptians also believed that hieroglyphic texts helped guide people in the afterlife, which explains why they are so often found in Egyptian tombs near the mummies.

Written language also helped improve commerce and trade. As transactions became larger, written records grew important for ensuring that the trades were fair and accurate. Keeping inventory by writing was far more precise than relying on memory. Not only did written language benefit business, but Mediterranean Sea trade played a key role in the spread of writing. As ships and caravans traveled to distant destinations, they carried with them these new ways of keeping records.

Today, the written records that these civilizations kept allow us to know more about the ancient cultures that lived beside the Mediterranean. Scholars examine Egyptian hieroglyphics, Greek and Roman texts, and other ancient texts for clues regarding how people lived in the ancient world. For instance, although nothing

Written language systems such as Egyptian hieroglyphics helped advance human civilization.

remains of Phoenician writing, we know that they imported huge amounts of papyrus from Egypt to the Phoenician port of Byblos. The word "Bible" ("the book") derives from the name Byblos.

Literature, Art, and Architecture

Over time, cities along the Mediterranean became wealthy trading centers. During the height of the Greek civilization, the port at Alexandria, Egypt, became a trading and cultural center. It was founded by Greek emperor Alexander the Great in 332 BCE, as he swept through the region in his conquest of Persia. The port had two harbors: one served trade from the Nile River; the other was a seaport for ships from throughout the Mediterranean and beyond.

Alexandria also hosted the ancient world's foremost library. Built during the third century BCE, the library was charged with trying to amass a collection of all the world's known books. It most likely never achieved that nearly impossible goal; it probably did, however, house every known piece of Greek literature, including precious works by Aristotle.

According to legend, building the collection was a serious undertaking. Every ship that entered the harbor of Alexandria was boarded, and Alexandrians took any books they found and added them to the library. Yet this was not piracy; they made copies of the books they'd taken and returned these copies, along with payment for the original.

No one knows for sure how many books were housed in the Library of Alexandria because the library was destroyed by fire early in the first century BCE. That tragedy erased many of the written records about life in the ancient world.

Athens and Rome also served as trade and cultural centers during the peak periods of the Greek and Roman empires, respectively. These cities drew visitors and ideas from across the ancient world. Greek and Roman artisans created art and architecture that still dazzle visitors two thousand years later. Examples of classic Greek architecture include the Parthenon, the Temple of Apollo, and the Theatre of Delphi. The influence of classic Greek architecture can still be seen in many of today's buildings. Courthouses and other public buildings, especially, often draw on features from classic Greek buildings. Meanwhile, Greek pottery and sculpture reflect an elegance and style that still appeal to artists today.

Roman architecture continued the legacy of Greek form, but Roman designers added their own design flair. Sites such as the Roman Colosseum and the

Pantheon still stand today and draw visitors from throughout the world. Also, because the Roman Empire at its peak extended across so much of Europe, Africa, and into Asia, its architecture became known worldwide. It then influenced the architectural styles of future buildings in those regions.

Another key center of culture and art in the ancient world stood at Constantinople. Situated between the Black Sea and the Mediterranean at the point where Asia and Europe meet, the city drew influence from both continents. Furthermore, for approximately a thousand years between 400 and 1450 CE, it served as a preeminent center for worldwide trade. The city retained the influence of the Romans who established it. At the same time, it drew from the Asians and Arabs who visited and traded there.

Constantinople also served as an end point for the famed Silk Road, which linked Asia and the Mediterranean in trade. The Silk Road began in China and stretched for more than 5,000 miles (8,046 km). The silk and other goods that it carried ended up in Constantinople, Damascus, and Tyre. From there, the goods and cultural influences they represented continued their journey across the Mediterranean throughout Europe and Africa. During its centuries of operation, the Silk Road brought together the cultures of East and West in ways that would forever alter both cultures.

The Renaissance

Between around 1300 and 1600 came a cultural reawakening in Europe known as the Renaissance. Classical knowledge from the Greeks, Byzantines, and other cultures helped fuel this time of artistic, cultural, and scientific discovery. Italy led the Renaissance, with

Leonardo da Vinci's Mona Lisa, *painted during the Renaissance, remains one of the world's most famous paintings today.*

cities such as Florence, Rome, and Venice becoming major centers for artists, sculptors, and scientists. Michelangelo created masterpieces such as painting the Sistine Chapel ceiling in Vatican City and his statue of David. Meanwhile, artist/scientist Leonardo da Vinci created works of art such as the *Mona Lisa* and scientific discoveries such as a sketch of a flying machine. The works of Michelangelo, Leonardo, and other Renaissance figures continue to stand as mighty achievements centuries later. The trade routes of the Mediterranean helped spread the fruits of the Renaissance to Africa, Asia, and beyond. The Renaissance also marked the transition between the Middle Ages and modern history.

Democratic Ideals

The Greeks established a form of government that included representation from many members of their society. The Romans also adopted this idea of a representative government, although they later were ruled by a series of emperors. As the Roman Empire expanded, it carried many of these Greco-Roman ideas to wider and wider areas. In the late 1700s, the founders of the United States used some of the Greco-Roman ideas about representative government as the basis for the nation's democratic government.

Religious Exchanges

Religion spread through trade routes in much the same way as culture. As merchants visited far-flung ports, they carried with them their various religions. And as civilizations such as the Egyptians, Greeks, and Romans expanded their lands through conquest they brought with them their beliefs and gods.

Trade and travel also helped spread the two major religions that dominate Europe, northern Africa, and western Asia: Christianity and Islam. In the centuries following the death of Christ around 30 CE, his disciples fanned out across western Asia and into Byzantium, Crete, Greece, and Rome. Meanwhile, after the death of Muhammad in 632 CE, Islam spread rapidly across North Africa and into Spain. Over time, the two religions, along with others, met.

Sometimes the religious exchanges were positive. Other times they brought tensions and even violence. For example, the Crusades pitted Christians against Muslims in a religious war that lasted for two centuries. Angered that Muslims controlled the holy city of Jerusalem, Pope Urban II urged that Christian armies gain control of the Holy Land. The Christians succeeded in capturing Jerusalem in 1099, and they established Christian strongholds in several places. One key stronghold lay in Acre in what is now northern Israel. Another lay in Constantinople. Located at the strategic intersection of Europe and Asia, it offered a launching point for Christian knights to march through Turkey and Syria to sacred sites in Lebanon and Israel.

Not surprisingly, Muslim forces resisted this Christian occupation. They launched a jihad, or holy war, to regain the territory. Battles between the Crusaders and Muslims continued for nearly two hundred years. In all, there were nine major crusades, as well as several minor ones. In 1291, the fall of the Christian stronghold at Acre, Israel, marked the end of the major fighting of the Crusades.

Muslim influence extended to other areas as well. Muslims ruled Spain for centuries, and they controlled much of northern Africa as well. In 1453, the Ottoman Turks, who were Muslims, captured Constantinople. This gave them control of the flow of silk, spices, and other trade goods coming from Asia.

A Shifting Balance

It is interesting to note how the balance of cultures and civilizations shifted over the centuries. At the beginning of recorded history, the greatest civilizations thrived in the southern and eastern edges of the Mediterranean with the Egyptians and Phoenicians. Then the center shifted to the north with the rise of the Minoans, Greeks, and Romans.

During the Dark Ages of Europe from around 500 to 1000 CE, influence once again shifted to the southern and eastern regions of the Mediterranean. The Byzantine Empire, centered in Constantinople, served as a center for knowledge and culture. Furthermore, it served as a meeting point between Asia and Europe, allowing for the interchange of ideas.

The Renaissance brought the focus back to the northern shores of the Mediterranean. The Renaissance began in Italy and spread to other European countries. Through trade, its effects were felt in Africa and Asia, too. Throughout modern history since the Renaissance, intellectual and artistic influences have become far less centered. Over time, worldwide travel became more common, and cultural influences became more blended. The rise of electronic media in recent decades has made knowledge and culture even more diffuse, as ideas and materials can come from anywhere at any time.

Effects on Daily Life

All in all, the trade routes of the Mediterranean had important effects on the daily lives of people in the Mediterranean region and beyond. The cultural, intellectual, and religious ideas that came from trade interchanges affected people's minds and souls. But the benefits of trade also affected their daily lives.

Food

The transport of wheat and other grain from rich growing areas improved the diet and health of people where grain did not grow well. People and countries that grew more grain than they could eat found that they could grow prosperous though trade. Grain could be traded for gold, spices, silk, and other luxury items. Thus, both sides benefited.

The transport of fruits also helped improve people's health. For instance, the ancient Egyptians and Greeks both discussed the disease of **scurvy**. Scurvy comes about from a lack of vitamin C in the diet. Scurvy causes fatigue and pain in the limbs. In some cases, it can be fatal. Foods that contain high concentrations of vitamin C include peppers, tomatoes, and broccoli. As foods such as these began being widely traded and consumed, the incidence of scurvy declined. Scurvy was a special problem for sailors on long sea voyages. Often they did not have access to nutritious foods while at sea.

Food and spices also changed people's eating and drinking habits. Apples originated in central Asia and traveled to Europe on the Silk Road. From there they spread worldwide. Spices such as cinnamon lent more flavor to food. Tea provided a new beverage to enjoy.

Clothing

Meanwhile, international trade changed the way that people dressed. The Silk Road got its name from the silk that traveled from China to Europe. Soft and lightweight, silk became a luxury item for nobles and wealthy Romans. Purple silk was so expensive that only

The Black Death

Gold. Silk. Spices. Over the centuries, traders crossing the Mediterranean Sea have carried all sorts of precious goods between Europe, Asia, and Africa. In the mid-1300s, traders traveling back from Asia brought an unwelcome guest: the Black Death. Carried by fleas living on rats, the disease may have traveled west on caravans along the Silk Road. It may also have come on ships. Once it reached the shores of the Mediterranean Sea, it quickly spread to major ports across Europe via trade vessels.

Also known as the plague, the Black Death brought fever and coughs, which would become bloody coughs. It also caused black spots of swelling that began in the groin or armpits and spread across the body. Most of the people who were infected died within a week. The bodies of the dead lay where they fell. Nobody wanted to touch the bodies to bury them for fear of catching the disease. Their fear was well founded. Over a period of less than a decade, the plague wiped out as many as half of all people living in Europe and Asia at the time.

rulers wore it. In fact, to this day, purple is associated with royalty. Over time, the price of regular silk came down enough that many people could afford it.

The clothing trade went both ways. Through the Silk Road, people in China and other parts of Asia were introduced to wool. Never having seen it before, the Chinese were drawn to carpets, blankets, and clothing made from this strong, warm fiber.

Housewares

Beginning in the Bronze Age, household items such as pots were important trade commodities. Bronze houseware was sturdier and lasted longer than previous kinds. The Greeks were masters at making pottery. Because they traveled and traded extensively, their pottery has been found at archaeological sites in northern Africa and western Asia.

Later, the Silk Road carried glass bottles east to China. The Chinese valued glass highly, as they had no industry for making glass of their own until the fifth century. Coming west was Chinese china, with its delicate texture and colorful designs. China cups, bowls, and dishes made elegant dinner settings at the dining tables of wealthy Europeans.

Money and Currency

At first, all trade in the ancient world was done by barter. Under this simple system, both trade partners would trade one set of goods for another. For example, a farmer might trade wheat or a goat for a bronze tool or pot. This method worked as long as each trade partner had something the other needed. Otherwise, the system broke down.

As trade became more extensive, the barter system no longer worked as effectively. People wanted a variety of goods, and it wasn't always convenient to barter for them. Or the buyer might not have a barter item that the seller wanted. To solve that problem, ancient civilizations invented **currency**. Early currency took different forms. The Egyptians used gold bars of a certain weight. Around 3000 BCE, the Mesopotamians developed the shekel. This unit of currency related both to a certain weight of barley and an equivalent amount of silver, bronze, or copper.

The Greeks and Romans used coins, as did other cultures of the time. Typically, governments produced the coins in order to control the amount made. Often the coins were stamped with the face of the current ruler. While barter still remains a form of trade today, coins brought a standardization that made doing business much easier as trade routes expanded to include multiple countries and cultures.

The Effect of the Suez Canal

Just over 100 miles (160.9 km) of land separates the Mediterranean Sea and the Red Sea. The idea of connecting those two bodies of water dates back to ancient times. The ancient Egyptians actually built a canal linking the Red Sea and the Nile Delta. However, after centuries of use, by medieval times it had fallen into disuse and was abandoned.

In the mid-1800s, the idea was revived. Building the canal, which stretches 120 miles (193.1 km) from Suez in the south to Port Said on the Mediterranean, took ten years. Work began in 1859, and the canal opened on November 17, 1869. The canal quickly became an

The Suez Canal served as a primary route for oil transport in the twentieth century, and it remains important today.

important corridor for international trade. It cut more than 4,000 miles (6,437.3 km) off the trip between the North Atlantic and northern Indian Ocean. Instead of traveling from Europe or the Americas all the way around the southern tip of Africa, ships could simply cross the Mediterranean and then go down the canal.

The Suez Canal contributed to a boom in world trade. It remained a strategic waterway through both World Wars, and after World War II, it served as a primary shipping lane for oil produced in the Middle East. Instability in the Middle East led to the Suez Canal being closed for several months in late 1956 and 1957. It closed for eight years between 1967 and 1975 as the result of conflict between Egypt and Israel, affecting the flow of oil worldwide.

By the time the canal reopened, its importance had greatly lessened. Oil companies had grown accustomed to using other routes for shipping. Furthermore, many of the new, larger oil tankers could no longer travel comfortably through the relatively narrow, shallow Suez Canal.

Chapter 6

The Future of Mediterranean Trade Routes

L ike the civilizations that use them, trade routes rise and fall in importance across the centuries. Some are replaced by more convenient routes. Others may lose favor if the resources that travel across them become depleted. Still others evolve over time, becoming something quite different than their starting point.

All of these factors have affected the Mediterranean Sea. Its trade routes were arguably the world's most important for many centuries because of the many great civilizations that dotted the Mediterranean's shores. The Egyptians, Greeks, Romans, Byzantines, and others all lent their influence to the region's development.

Over the centuries, improved shipbuilding techniques opened up larger oceans such as the

Opposite: Tourism, especially using cruise ships, plays an important role in the economy of the Mediterranean today.

Atlantic Ocean and Pacific Ocean. This gradually reduced reliance on Mediterranean trade routes. Further, after the Renaissance came the rise of countries in western Europe. Then exploration across the Atlantic Ocean led to the opening of trade with North America and South America. Trade routes crossing the Atlantic grew in importance.

Still, the Mediterranean remained prominent throughout the twentieth century. It served as a strategic center for the movement of troops and supplies in both World War I and World War II. In World War II, battles raged for more than two and a half years as the United States and its allies fought against the Germans and Italians for control of North Africa. Once the Allies achieved victory, bases in North Africa served as the launching point for a campaign across the Mediterranean to invade Sicily and Italy. Control of North Africa also ensured that the Allies maintained access to oil from the Middle East.

After the war, oil continued to be a key commodity. As dependence on automobile and air travel increased throughout the world, global demand for oil skyrocketed. Much of that oil came from the Middle East and northern Africa. A large percentage of that oil traveled up the Suez Canal and across the Mediterranean before crossing the Atlantic Ocean, much of it destined for the United States. Opened in 1869 after ten years of construction, the Suez Canal connects the Mediterranean Sea and the Red Sea.

A Shipping Revolution

Following World War II, trade became increasingly globalized. According to World Ocean Review, since the 1950s until nearly 2010, the growth rate of international trade was almost consistently twice that of overall economic activity. World trade now accounts for 45 percent of the global gross domestic product (GDP).

Over the centuries, the technology of shipbuilding evolved. Ships grew bigger, sturdier, and faster. Motors replaced sails as the primary means of propulsion. Still, for centuries, the means of carrying and loading cargo remained pretty much the same. Cargo traveled in barrels, sacks, and crates. This "break-bulk" form of shipping was difficult and labor intensive. Crews had to load and unload each individual piece of cargo by hand. It was backbreaking, labor-intensive work, and it was also inefficient. Ships might spend more time in port being loaded and unloaded than they spent at sea.

In 1956, Malcolm McLean of North Carolina devised a system of **containerization** that used large, standardized rectangular containers for shipping cargo. These containers are far easier to load and unload from ships. They can be stacked to make more efficient use of space on board the vessel. This idea revolutionized the shipping industry and made it much more efficient.

Containers come in standard sizes of 20 feet, 40 feet, 45 feet, 48 feet, and 53 feet (6.1 meters, 12.2 meters, 13.7 meters, 14.6 meters, 16.1 meters). These standard sizes make loading, unloading, and storage much more efficient. By trimming the time spent in port, ships can make more trips over the course of a year. This leads to faster overall delivery times and substantial cost savings.

The 20-foot (6.1-m) container was initially the standard size. Its use led to the development of the term "twenty-foot equivalent unit" (TEU) as the standard unit for measuring amounts of material

Large container ships can carry thousands of twenty-foot equivalent units (TEUs) at a time.

shipped. Today the 40-foot (12.2-m) container is the most commonly used. The TEU remains the common term for expressing the volume of goods shipped, however.

According to the nonprofit World Shipping Council, there are currently containers totaling 34 million TEUs in the global fleet. Today, container ships carry about 60 percent of the value of all goods shipped by sea.

These giant ships carry thousands of TEU shipping containers at a time. The world's largest container ship, the *CSCL Globe*, launched in late 2014. Measuring 1,312 feet long (399.8 m), or more than the length of four football fields, the ship can carry a staggering 19,000 TEU shipping containers at a single time. But even as more of these giant ships go into service, global trade growth stagnated following the 2008–2009 financial crisis. With increased numbers of ships to fill and a world economy that remains slow, the profits for major container shipping lines tumbled.

The Mediterranean remains important for shipping today. Much of the trade occurs among ports on the Mediterranean. This type of trade, where ships don't have to cross entire oceans, is called short sea shipping. For instance, the Mediterranean Shipping Company operates nearly five hundred vessels sailing two hundred routes. According to Eurostat, the shipping of goods between main European Union ports and Mediterranean ports totaled 582 million tons (527.9 million tonnes) in 2014. This made Mediterranean ports the largest single destination for EU shipping, ahead of the North Sea and the Baltic Sea.

For more than two thousand years, the Greeks have been known for their love of the sea. Their skill and daring as sailors was renowned throughout the ancient world. Even today, Greeks play a major role in worldwide shipping. According to the United Nations Conference on Trade and Development (UNCTAD), Greece ranked as the world's leading ship-owning country in 2015. Greek owners accounted for more than 16 percent of the world's fleet. Other top nations for ship owning include Japan, China, Germany, and Singapore. In 2015, the global merchant fleet totaled 89,464 vessels.

Meanwhile, according to UNCTAD, Morocco and Egypt rank among the top three "best connected" countries for shipping in Africa, along with South Africa. Connectedness refers to a coastal country's access to the global network of containerized cargo

Like hundreds of ships on the seas today, this one flies a Greek flag.

shipping lines. Morocco's strategic location at the intersection of the Mediterranean Sea and the North Atlantic Ocean ensures that a steady stream of shipping flows through its waters. Likewise, Egypt benefits from its control of the Suez Canal as a vital link between the Mediterranean and the Red Sea.

Despite recent softness in the shipping market, the long-term future for shipping throughout the Mediterranean remains bright. There will always be worldwide demand for the goods transported across the Mediterranean, both regionally and throughout the world.

A Top Tourist Destination

A cruise ship drops anchor at Santorini, Greece. Hundreds of tourists from all over the world descend the gangplank, staring in awe at rows of whitewashed homes standing in stark contrast to the jet black hills of the volcanic island. Soon they will roam the black pebble beaches and explore fertile vineyards. They will marvel at ancient ruins dating back thousands of years.

This type of scene takes place every single day at ports throughout the Mediterranean. On any given week, dozens of cruise ships carrying tens of thousands of passengers sail its waters. According to Newsmax.com, the Mediterranean ranks among the world's top six cruise routes. The most popular ports include Athens and Santorini in Greece; Barcelona, Spain; Dubrovnik, Croatia; Istanbul, Turkey; Lisbon, Portugal; Rome and Venice in Italy; Valletta, Malta; and ports along the French Riviera. These ports offer a rich array of history, culture, and opportunities for sightseeing.

Not only can tourists explore some of the world's most vibrant cities, but they can also see artifacts of the great civilizations that have inhabited the region since the beginning of recorded time. In Greece, they can see the Acropolis, where three magnificent temples stand dating back to the fifth century BCE. They can also see the islands of Crete and Santorini, which features the archaeological site of Akrotiri, an ancient Minoan settlement.

In Italy, tourists enjoy seeing remnants of the mighty Roman Empire. These include the Colosseum and the Roman Forum. Istanbul features many sacred sites for both Christians and Muslims, including the Basilica Cistern and several historic mosques.

Tourists in Istanbul also flock to the Grand Bazaar, one of the largest and oldest covered markets in the world. The bazaar, which includes five thousand shops

The Grand Bazaar in Istanbul ranked as the world's most popular tourist attraction in 2014.

spread over more than sixty streets, drew more than ninety million visitors in 2014. This made it the world's most popular tourist attraction. The bazaar dates back to 1455, and it retains the unique flavor it enjoys from sitting perched at the intersection of Europe and Asia.

Today, visitors to the Grand Bazaar will find some of the same goods that first drew merchants more than five hundred years ago: silk from China, Turkish ceramics and carpets, spices, and more. They also enjoy the same thrill of bartering with merchants that traders experienced when the bazaar first opened.

Statistics from the Cruise Lines International Association (CLIA) place Europe as the world's second-leading cruise destination in 2014, ranking only behind the Caribbean. According to the CLIA, 5.85 million passengers embarked on cruises from a European port in 2014. Many of these ports were along the Mediterranean. The industry accounted for 350,000 jobs across Europe. More than 13 million passengers embarked or disembarked from the top ten Mediterranean European ports in 2014. Popular North African and Middle Eastern ports along the Mediterranean include Tangier, Morocco; Tripoli, Libya; Alexandria, Egypt; and Tel-Aviv and Haifa in Israel.

Alexandria, Egypt, remains a popular stop for cruise ships. Founded by Alexander the Great and home to Cleopatra, the city served as a cultural and intellectual center of the ancient world. Today it offers a rich mix of historical charm and modern amenities. Founded around 300 BCE, the Library at Alexandria served as a repository of knowledge in the ancient world. The library was destroyed by fire around 48 BCE while the city was occupied by the Roman forces of Julius Caesar. The huge modern Bibliotheca Alexandrina opened in 2002 and ranks as one of the world's great libraries.

From Alexandria, many tourists venture inland to the pyramids. The Great Pyramid of Giza stands as the last remaining member of the Seven Wonders of the Ancient World. At 481 feet (146.6 m) tall, the Great Pyramid stood for many centuries as the tallest structure in the world until the building of modern skyscrapers. Visitors admire those ancient pyramids and marvel at how they were constructed over a period of decades by thousands of paid workers. The Sphinx, with its human head and lion's body, stands nearby.

A Closer Look at Containerization

In the 1950s, Malcolm McLean of North Carolina ran a small shipping company. He knew first-hand how difficult it was to load and unload cargo and how much space was wasted. McLean went on to pioneer the system of containerization. This involved using cranes to lift large, standard-sized containers directly from trains or trucks onto flatbed ships for their ocean journey. When they reached their destinations, the cargo could be unloaded the same way and loaded back onto trains or trucks for delivery. A key part of the system is having the same cargo in the same container transported by different means; this is called **intermodalism**.

Made of aluminum or steel, the standard-sized containers stack easily, maximizing precious space aboard cargo ships. Depending on what goods they are carrying, these containers may open from the top or sides. Tank containers convey liquids such as chemicals or wine. Refrigerated containers convey items that might spoil during transit, such as fruits. Improved shipping methods and faster shipping times help account for the wider variety of foods now available in grocery stores year round. Dates from northern Africa and olives from Italy can now reach North America and other destinations faster than ever before. With loading and unloading time at the ports reduced, they arrive in stores faster and fresher.

Malcolm McLean of North Carolina pioneered the system of containerization that revolutionized modern shipping.

Scenes like this one explain why the Mediterranean Sea is so popular among tourists.

People interested in religious history enjoy cruising to Israel. After disembarking from the port at Jerusalem (Ashdod), tourists can take the hour trip inland and visit the most sacred places of three religions. In one day, they can see the Western Wall (or Wailing Wall), a sacred site for Jews. They can visit the Church of the Holy Sepulchre, which is said to mark the site of Jesus's crucifixion, burial, and resurrection. They can see the Al-Aqsa Mosque; it is from this area that Muslims believe the Prophet Muhammad was taken up to the heavens to see the signs of God. The mosque sits on the Temple Mount, which has significance to all three religions.

Storied Past, Steady Present, Bright Future

Like all trade routes, the Mediterranean has experienced ups and downs over the centuries. But through all of the changes, it has remained a vital link between Asia, Africa, Europe, and beyond. Bordered by more than twenty countries representing Europe, Africa, and the Middle East, the Mediterranean seems certain to remain a vibrant part of world trade for the foreseeable future. Its northern shores host countries at the southern end of the European Union. In 2014, the EU accounted for 15 percent of world trade. Imports and exports together totaled more than $3 trillion, ranking it with China and the United States as world leaders.

Meanwhile, the African nations along the southern reaches of the Mediterranean remain rich in natural resources. Looking at the whole of Africa, Libya, Angola, and Algeria all rank among the top twenty oil-producing countries in the world. Together, they produced more than 4.2 million barrels of oil per day in 2014. The Mediterranean remains a key means for transporting that oil to other countries in the region and throughout the world.

Looking forward, Mediterranean trade routes seem certain to have a bright future. The sea's strategic location between Africa, Asia, and Europe makes it a vital connection between the world's three most populous continents. Between them, these three continents house approximately 6.5 billion of the world's 7.5 billion people. While past performance does not necessarily predict future trends, the routes' steadiness over centuries of change suggests that they will remain important in the future.

Glossary

alloy A metal made by combining two or more elements.

annexed Added to an existing territory.

commodity A material or product that is bought and sold.

containerization A method of shipping that involves putting all of the cargo in standardized rectangular containers that can be stacked easily.

cuneiform The characters used in the writing system of ancient Mesopotamia.

currency A kind of money a group of people or country uses.

domesticated Describes a species of animal that has been trained to be tame.

galley A long, slender ship propelled primarily by rowing.

hubs Centers for activity.

intermodalism The process of having the same cargo container transported by different means.

mariners Another word for sailors, used more in ancient times.

monopoly The exclusive control over something.

nomads People who move from place to place with no permanent home.

periplus A Greek document listing ports and coastal landmarks that ancient sailors used for navigation.

pictographs Pictures that serve as symbols for words or phrases.

pillaged To have robbed violently.

propulsion The action of moving forward, as with a ship.

Renaissance A period of heightened interest in art, literature, and learning that spread through Europe beginning in the fourteenth century.

scurvy A disease caused by a lack of vitamin C in the diet; it causes exhaustion, swelling, and sometimes death.

sedentary Staying or living in one place.

siege The surrounding of a town in order to make it surrender by cutting its supplies.

sledge A vehicle mounted on runners, often used to carry loads over sand, snow, or ice.

trireme A type of galley warship used by the Phoenicians, Greeks, and Romans.

Further Information

Books

D'Amato, Raffaele, and Andrea Salimbeti. *Sea Peoples of the Bronze Age Mediterranean c. 1400 BC–1000 BC*. Oxford, UK: Osprey Books, 2015.

Fullman, Joseph. *DK Eyewitness Books: Ancient Civilizations*. New York, NY: DK Books, 2013.

Millward, James A. *The Silk Road: A Very Short Introduction*. Oxford, UK: Oxford University Press, 2013.

World History: Student Edition Ancient Civilizations Through the Renaissance. New York, NY: Holt McDougal, 2010.

Websites

Comparisons Between Ancient Greece and Ancient Rome
http://ancienthistory.about.com/od/greecevsrome/ss/
GreecevsRome.htm#step.
Examine similarities and differences between ancient Greece and ancient Rome in eight key areas.

Secrets of Ancient Navigators
http://www.pbs.org/wgbh/nova/ancient/secrets-of-ancient-navigators.html.
Learn more about how ancient sailors managed to navigate the waters of the Mediterranean Sea.

How Ancient Trade Changed the World
http://www.livescience.com/4823-ancient-trade-changed-world.htm.
Take a closer look at the basics of early trade.

Videos

"Fall of Constantinople"
http://www.history.com/topics/ancient-history/byzantine-empire/videos
Learn more about the end of the Byzantine Empire in this short video from the History Channel.

"Wrecks of the Abyss"
http://nationalgeographic.org/media/ancient-mariners-mediterranean/
Follow along as archaeologists dive for clues about early Mediterranean trade.

Bibliography

Abulafia, David, ed. *The Mediterranean in History*. Los Angeles, CA: Getty Publications, 2003.

Anderson, Marge. "Trade: The Renaissance." Big Site of History. Retrieved November 11, 2016. http://bigsiteofhistory.com/trade-the-renaissance/.

Boxer, Baruch, and Mostafa Moh. Salah. "Mediterranean Sea." Encyclopaedia Britannica. Retrieved October 15, 2016. https://www.britannica.com/place/Mediterranean-Sea.

Carr, Karen Eva. "Greek Boats and Ships." Quatr.us. Retrieved November 8, 2016. http://quatr.us/greeks/science/sailing/boats.htm.

Cartwright, Mark. "Trade in Ancient Greece." Ancient History Encyclopedia. Retrieved November 3, 2016. http://www.ancient.eu/article/115/.

Cruise Lines International Association. *The Cruise Industry: Contribution of Cruise Tourism to the Economies of Europe 2015 Edition*. 2015.

Encyclopaedia Britannica. "Caravan: Desert Transport." Retrieved October 20, 2016. https://www.britannica.com/topic/caravan-desert-transport.

Frank, Irene M., and David M. Brownstone. *To the Ends of the Earth: The Great Travel and Trade Routes of Human History*. New York, NY: Facts on File Publications, 1984.

Gore, Rick. "Who Were the Phoenicians?" *National Geographic*, October 2004. http://ngm.nationalgeographic.com/features/world/asia/lebanon/phoenicians-text/2.

Ifland, Peter. "The History of the Sextant." University of Coimbra. Retrieved November 14, 2016. http://www.mat.uc.pt/~helios/Mestre/Novemb00/H61iflan.htm.

Jarus, Owen. "How Were the Egyptian Pyramids Built?" Live Science. Retrieved October 24, 2016. http://www.livescience.com/32616-how-were-the-egyptian-pyramids-built-.html.

McLaughlin, Raoul. *The Roman Empire and the Silk Routes*. South Yorkshire, UK: Pen & Sword History, 2016.

Parker, Philip, ed. *The Great Trade Routes: A History of Cargoes and Commerce Over Land and Sea*. Annapolis, MD: Naval Institute Press, 2012.

Quick, Darren. "World's Largest Capacity Container Ship Embarks on Maiden Voyage." New Atlas, 2014. http://newatlas.com/cscl-globe-worlds-largest-container-ship-hyundai/35102/.

Tyldesley, Joyce. "The Private Lives of the Pyramid-builders." BBC History. Retrieved November 1, 2016. http://www.bbc.co.uk/history/ancient/egyptians/pyramid_builders_01.shtml.

Tyson, Peter. "Secrets of Ancient Navigators." NOVA. Retrieved November 1, 2016. http://www.pbs.org/wgbh/nova/ancient/secrets-of-ancient-navigators.html.

Williams, Elizabeth. "Trade and Commercial Activity in the Byzantine and Early Islamic Middle East." Metropolitan Museum of Art. Retrieved October 26, 2016. http://www.metmuseum.org/toah/hd/coin/hd_coin.htm.

Yule, Colonel Sir Henry, ed. *The Book of Ser Marco Polo: The Venetian Concerning Kingdoms and Marvels of the East, Volumes I and II*. London, UK: John Murray, 1903.

Index

Page numbers in **boldface** are illustrations. Entries in **boldface** are glossary terms.

Africa, 4, 6–7, 9, 24–25, 27–28, 36, 38, 43, 45, 47, 51, 58, 62, 64–66, 68–69, 71, 74, 77, 81, 82, 85
Alexandria, 5–6, 22, **23**, 25, 53, 60–61, 81
alloy, 32
annexed, 45
architecture, 61–62
artwork, **40, 60**, 60–62
Asia, 4, 6, 24–27, 33–34, 47, 50, 58, 62, 64–69, 80, 85
Atlantic Ocean, 4, 6, 27–28, 39, 51, 74, 78

bartering, 35, 69–70, 80
Black Death, 68
bronze/Bronze Age, **30**, 31–32, 42, 48, 69
Byzantine Empire, 6, 25–26, 45–47, 62, 65–66, 73
camels, 9, **14**, 14–15

Cape of Good Hope, 6, 27, 47
Carthage, 24, 35, 43, 45
China, 6, 15, 22, 25, 33–36, 49, 52–53, 62, 67–69, 77, 80, 85
clothing, 67–69
commodity, 7, 25, 31, 33–34, 36–37, 39, 47, 69, 74
Constantinople, 6, 15, 25–27, 34, 45–47, **46**, 62, 65–66
containerization, 75–76, 77–78, 82–83, **82–83**
container ship, 75–78, **76**
Crete, 19, 24, 32, 43, 65
Crusades, 65
cultural influences of trade, 57–64
cuneiform, 11
currency, 69–70
Cyprus, 19, 24–25, 36, 43

da Gama, Vasco, 27
democratic ideals, 64
deserts, 14–15, **14–15**
Dias, Bartolomeu, 6, 27
domesticated, 9

Egypt, 7, 36, 42, 71,
    77–78, 81
    ancient, 5, 11–13,
        18–20, 24–25,
        31–32, 41–43, 45,
        50, 53, 57–61, 64,
        66–67, 70, 73
Europe, 4, 6–7, 25–28, 32,
    45, 47, 52, 62, 65–68,
    74, 80–81, 85
explorers, 48–50

fish/fishing, 31, 37
food, 67

galley, 20, 47
Genoa, 6, 25–26, 47
grains, 31, 33, 36, 50, 55,
    67
Grand Bazaar, 79–80, **80**
Great Pyramid, **8**, 11–13,
    22, 81
Greece, 77–79
    ancient, 5–6, 13, 19–21,
        24–26, 29, 33, 43–45,
        48, 53, 59–62, 64–67,
        69–70, 73, 79

hieroglyphics, 11, 42,
    58–59, **60**
housewares, 69
hubs, 6, 45
intermodalism, 82

Israel, 4, 7, 24, 32, 65,
    71, 81, 84
Istanbul, 79–80, **80**
Italy, 7, 17, 20, 24, 29,
    32, 47, 62–63, 66, 74,
    79, 82

Lebanon, 4, 18, 24, 32,
    41, 43, 58, 65
Library of Alexandria,
    60–61, 81
Lighthouse at Alexandria,
    5, 22–23, **23**, 53
lighthouses, 22–23, 53
literature, 60–61

mariners, 17, 21–22, 53
Mediterranean Sea and
    trade routes, **73**, **84**
    about Mediterranean,
        4–7
    dangers of sailing,
        28–29, 50–51, 53, 55
    effects of, 57–71
    evolution of, 17–27
    future of, 73–85
    goods traded, 31–39
    maps, **5**, **18**
    trade before the
        Mediterranean routes,
        9–15
    merchants, 25, 34–35,
        53–55, **54–55**

Mesopotamia, 9–11, **10**, 70
Middle East, 9, 39, 42, 45, 74, 81, 85
Minoans, 19, 24, 32, 42–43, 66, 79
Mona Lisa, **63**, 64
monopoly, 34
Morocco, 4, 35, 50, 77–78, 81

navigation, 17, 19, 21–22, 24, 29, 53
nomads, 9–10

Odyssey, 5, 29, 48
oil, 7, 27, 31, 37–39, 42, 71, 74, 85
oil tanker, 7, **38**, 39, 71

Parthenon, **56**, 61–62
periplus, 21
Phoenicians, 5, 20–21, 24–25, 32, 43, 53, 58, 60, 66
pictographs, 11
pillaged, 50
pirates, 50–53, **51**, 55
Polo, Marco, 6, 26, 48–50, **49**, 52
propulsion, 19–20, 47, 75

Red Sea, 27, 42, 48, 70, 74, 78
religion, 59, 64–65, 79, 84
Renaissance, 6, 26, 47, 62–64, 66, 74
Roman Empire, 5–6, 20, 23, 25, 33–34, 37, 44–46, 50, 53, 59, 61–62, 64–66, 70, 73, 79, 81

sailors, 53–54, 77
scurvy, 67
Scylla and Charybdis, legend of, **28**, 29
sedentary, 10
Seven Wonders of the Ancient World, 5, 22, 81
ships/shipbuilding, **16**, 17–20, **38**, 42, 47, **72**, 73–75, **76**, 78–79
siege, 33
silk, 4, 6, 15, 25–26, 31, 33–36, 47, 50, 55, 65, 67–69, 80
Silk Road, 6, 15, 22, 25–26, 34–37, 47–49, 55, 62, 67–69
slavery, 4, 31, 36, 50
sledge, 11
Spain, 4, 7, 20, 24–25, 27, 32, 36, 45, 65, 79

spices, 4, 26, 34, 36–37,
    50, 55, 65, 67–68, 80
Suez Canal, 7, 27, 39, 42,
    70–71, **71**, 74, 78
Sumerians, 10–11
Syria, 4–5, 9–10, 19,
    24–25, 32, 36, 43, 65

tin, 31, 31–32
tourism, 7, **72**, 78–84
trireme, **16**, 20

Venice, 6, 25–27, 47–49,
    63

World Wars, 6–7, 71, 74
written language, 10–11,
    58–60

About the Author

John Micklos Jr. is an award-winning education journalist and the author of more than thirty books for children and young adults. His work includes poetry books for young readers, history books for elementary students, and history and biography titles for middle school and high school students. He also contributed to National Geographic Kids' popular book *125 True Stories of Amazing Pets*. His newest books include *The Sound in the Basement* and *Beach Fun: Poems of Surf and Sand*, picture books published by First State Press. John has done K–12 school visits in several states and has spoken at the national conferences of the International Reading Association and the National Council of Teachers of English, as well as at state reading conferences in New York, Pennsylvania, New Jersey, Maryland, and Delaware. Learn more at John's website, www.JohnMicklosWriter.com.